Meredith Stricker's *SENTIENCE* is a radical expression of loving solidarity with Being, nature's unbounded ground. Fulfilling the literal premise of ecopoetry, *oikos* and *poiesis*, these poems fashion a home "at the non-carceral edge of dreams" where man-made boundaries dissolve: "your interior my interior the wilderness' interior inside a word." Hers is a politics of an ensouled world where "language is / both inside / and outside the body / intra-species, polyphonic." This is visionary work, its ecstasy derived from the gnosis of delving ever more deeply into ecological relation, its grief an outcome of bearing witness to relation's devastation.

BRIAN TEARE, AUTHOR OF *POEM BITTEN BY A MAN*

The poems in Meredith Stricker's "Hazardous Materials" series rest on a bedrock of notation. The borrowed lines from varied sources: Kafka, Coleridge, Dickinson, Benjamin, Bill Viola, to list only a few are sometimes used as epigraphs, sometimes as scaffolding, and frequently as echoes that argue that all utterance is interconnected. While the poems traffic in lyric beauty, it's never at the cost of pretending the real world with its real ruin doesn't exist: oil spills and waste water infused with prescription drug residues, "the rawness / the mess / the Veiling of beauty // lost in twigs, 'cured' of language, unfinished and starry." I have great confidence in these poems, in their inclusivity and their formal reach. Language is never more than a fractured mirror of world but these poems come closer than most to capturing the complexity of what is in front of us.

MARY JO BANG, CITATION FOR WORK IN *SENTIENCE* AWARDED THE IOWA REVIEW POETRY PRIZE

Meredith Stricker's brilliant *SENTIENCE* gives us the architectures of the page as a Muschampian museum in our mind, a paradise for saying and seeing. The language and the form are as keenly wound as the honeycomb housing bees. Saying, here, also proclaims loss. Seeing comes in Deleuze/Guattari-like frames, sometimes indexical, sometimes asymmetrical, all rhizomic. Word and image become entanglements where science, dream, and destruction must be witnessed, downloaded, then actionized. With masterful poetic pacing, Stricker's collection accelerates on a neogothic-modern event plane from one page to another and one mind-space to another with an auditory generational resonance. Stricker flames our discontent by summoning Beuys as a fiction-maker and Shelley as the imagist inventor of the inferno of human nature. On whole, *SENTIENCE* is a love song for survivors, an argument for the soul. For Stricker, beauty dwells in words as if isomers could say, see, and name. *SENTIENCE* burns with a call for a collective performance, an exchange of awe in praise of lyrical resistance.

CYDNEY PAYTON, CURATOR-AT-LARGE, FORMER DIRECTOR AND CHIEF CURATOR OF THE MUSEUM OF CONTEMPORARY ART DENVER

Meredith Stricker's *SENTIENCE* is a poetic embodiment that intersects creatives from across literary and philosophical disciplines, while inviting readers to imagine how the imagination might encompass more than we ever conceived. Her language is being itself, while simultaneously being a language we all think, feel and experience. It is a wonder how she can navigate through invisible universes that make one feel nostalgic. Her eloquent "magic-ifs" lead us to ask if anyone has ever envisioned how the political is as much spiritual as it is not? This collection clearly demonstrates hers is a singular voice echoing the many "we's" each of us contains.

GEORGE EMILIO SANCHEZ IS A BROOKLYN-BASED WRITER AND PERFORMANCE ARTIST, TOURING THE U.S. WITH *IN THE COURT OF THE CONQUEROR*

SENTIENCE

Cover art by Thom Cowen
Cover typeface: Aptos

Interior design by Laura Joakimson and Meredith Stricker
Interior typefaces: Perpetua and Minion

Library of Congress Cataloging-in-Publication Data

Names: Stricker, Meredith author
Title: Sentience / Meredith Stricker.
Description: Oakland, California : Omnidawn Publishing, 2026. | Summary: "With this collection, poet and artist Meredith Stricker considers questions about personhood, belonging, property, and ownership within interdependent living cultural systems. Looking beyond humans alone, she considers whether animals dream, who our relations are, what interior lives are held within words, and whether the world is truly alive to us today or if it is simply something we experience through screens. The poems track bee swarms and hazardous waste, separation walls, and diatoms. They are intently visual, aural, and spatial, tracing the dendritic forms of trees and fractal coastlines and the symmetries of biomorphic animal patterns. They highlight non-artificial, non-extractive intelligences in sharp contrast to the rise of AI. Informed by biosemiotics, SENTIENCE arises from Stricker's continuing multidisciplinary work and architectural habitat restoration in Big Sur and her performance collaborations with musicians, composers, artists, and beekeepers"-- Provided by publisher.
Identifiers: LCCN 2026020237 (print) | LCCN 2026020238 (ebook) | ISBN 9781632432292 trade paperback | ISBN 9781632432353 epub
Subjects: LCGFT: Poetry
Classification: LCC PS3619.T747 S46 2026 (print) | LCC PS3619.T747 (ebook) | DDC 811/.6--dc23/eng/20260415
LC record available at https://lccn.loc.gov/2026020237
LC ebook record available at https://lccn.loc.gov/2026020238

Published by Omnidawn Publishing, Oakland, California
www.omnidawn.com
10 9 8 7 6 5 4 3 2 1
ISBN: 978-1-63243-229-2

SENTIENCE

MEREDITH STRICKER

OMNIDAWN PUBLISHING
OAKLAND, CALIFORNIA
2026

PREVIOUS BOOKS

Rewild, Dorset Prize, Tupelo Press

Our Animal, Omnidawn Open Book Competition Award

Tenderness Shore, National Poetry Series Award, LSU Press

Alphabet Theater, performance poetry & visual art, Wesleyan University Press

CHAPBOOKS

Anemochore, Newfound Press, Four Quartets Award finalist

mistake, Caketrain Press Award

FOR THOM

“Crying faith / In this in which the wild deer
Startle, and stare out”

GEORGE OPPEN

SENTIENCE

I DREAMED I WAS A BOOK

"We must consider speech before it is spoken."
MERLEAU-PONTY

Sometimes a soul does not know it is a book when living
whose pages can never be completed in a final, perfect, finished sense
but are continually translating themselves just as leaves fall and translate
the forest, chaparral, grassland in succession and no street adheres
to its past self, just as leaves fall and leaves love us and traffic is humanity
surging out of the boundaries of its skin

stars are Being
stars are being counted
barbed wire in stars
black seed in stars
itemized thoughts
foreheads imprinted
I dreamed I was a book
the book is Heisenberg
I open and close my hand
a bird flies to the sun
the book writes itself in me
never once remains the same
acceleration of stars
their noise burns
the inner ear
lie down
lie down
in listening
stars

Do animals DREAM?

"Selves are signs. Lives are thoughts. Semiosis is alive.
And the world is thereby animate.

'We' are not the only kind of 'we'".

EDUARDO KOHN, *HOW FORESTS THINK: TOWARD AN ANTHROPOLOGY BEYOND THE HUMAN*

DEAR ANIMATE:

We were talking about the difference between "kin" and "kindred" —
Do we include those outside our family, our species?
Who includes us, who do we include? trees with their oxygen
out-breath? bees? those who remain stateless, undocumented or "illegal"?
the "inanimate" — rocks and rivers? What happens to a culture
that narrows and nuclears its sense of family?

Cecilia Vicuña says "in her performance Theresa Cha would give
the audience white cards that read 'distant relative'.
Rocks, water, fire are also our relatives."

dear distant. dear relative

we are the shadows of
our animals

DO ANIMALS DREAM?

[redacted], science confir[redacted]anim[redacted]rea[redacted]
[redacted]animals c[redacted]m s[redacted]
does [redacted]
do I dream animals[redacted]
[redacted]m I their scie[redacted]
[redacted]estigial w[redacted]
[redacted]ny am[redacted] lungs
[redacted]s evo[redacted] a dream
[redacted]s phy[redacted]ny a dream

is m[redacted] *telos*
[redacted]en[redacted]ots
[redacted]n I two [redacted] deer
[redacted]on fevered fre[redacted]
[redacted]s my mouth a[redacted]oth in lampli[redacted]

[redacted]s my mind [redacted]te[redacted]liding with the[redacted] of blue ja[redacted]
and [redacted] the [redacted]ite[redacted]e sky betwee[redacted]

DO ANIMALS DREAM?

yes, science confirms animals dream
but do animals confirm science
does science dream
do I dream animals
am I their science
who dreamt my vestigial wings
my amphibian lungs
is evolution a dream
is phylogeny a dream
is God science
is my digital *Telos*
swift enough for ocelots
am I two Reverdy deer
on fevered freeway edge
is my mouth a moth in lamplight
is my mind a swarm of termites colliding with the beaks of blue jays
and my soul the mind of termites the sky between

wearing trees our brains shrouded with hawks buses roar
our caves fill with missiles our ears long to open
and stroke the fur of our plant bodies

the tongue a meadow fluorescing

LIE DOWN

the animal is weary, the anima
        packed into shipping containers

the soul is tired of people
saying who is not
allowed into heaven
the pitiable the poor
the unloved
the unwashed
the unshriven
undocumented
ancestors
all animals
anteaters
moths, microbes
even radiant
Medusa jellyfish
are not allowed
the soul
is tired of this paradise
of downloading
and upgrading
and forwarding
the soul's GIF
is tired of waving
its Sisyphus arms

lie down soul and rest on this cool riverbed
water lapping the mud of minnows

THE LIFE OF A WORD DARK TO ITSELF

at the non-carceral edge of dreams
 the tundra of a word, its unslaked thirst

if the soul
is this foreigner
hidden in me
if the soul is
innermost wind-
blown crowds
of leaves
if the soul
is placenta
a seed a cloud
in collusion with matter
if the soul is panic-stricken
if the soul is unfenced land
then spillways and forests
their velocities, their philosophies
our nervous system burning like a codex-sun
before and after the mysteries

black island of letters unvoiced black statues of wild birds
untraceable black iris of black sight black Iset of crowning night
black wash of stars gone into the lens of leaving
gone into black fields receiving

THE BRIGHTNESS OF THE ANIMAL

"embedded in the visible that hides them"
JEAN-CHRISTOPHE BAILLY

there was the flaring
of bodies in sun's path the brightness
of an awkward and prehistoric body
with wide-sieved mouth, wider than Jerusalem
pelican folded like a dark arrow plunges
without hesitation into the abode of water
60,000 pelicans once sheltered in Gulf rookeries
now thousands of dead birds
the young emaciated and abandoned
to the spreading sheen of oil
dense with dispersants
water silver-black as feldspar
waves like rapid eye movements
in waters fat and rancid
an oil slick unfurls like silk
gives birth to blinded crabs
seabirds whose wings
are pressed back, useless
our industry, our tourists
sores on their skin
mouths wide open
bright words bright day
bright orchard bright water
bright boat bright cloud

WHEN RIVERS ARE GRANTED PERSONHOOD

do corporations dream in clear calm morning
threaded by contrails

& if a corporation is a person but not a migrant
does the corporation have a soul but not

the chicken I eat nor the river downstream
from the person of the corporation

if a corporation is a person does it wake up
in dread sometimes like a person does

and cannot get out of its chair unassisted
when its legs no longer work so well its eyes no longer see

the corporation falls down goes to its first day of class
trembling with excitement and terror it gets depressed

gets a pink slip a tumor it is sad it is compassionate
it lies on the ground ecstatic seeing a young pine tree

and one day it lies down on the ground and gives
its body back to the vast, undocumented microbial ferment

breaking down into particles of lyric
—
the sentence, ~~a sentence~~ — a sentience

when rivers are granted personhood
are you more or less sentient than whales

do you hear them laid out and skinned
against the bow of oblivion

hunted and plundered then rendered
yet still curious about us

—

when rivers are granted personhood
we are mortal like glaciers

and if trees

have no soul

then neither
do we

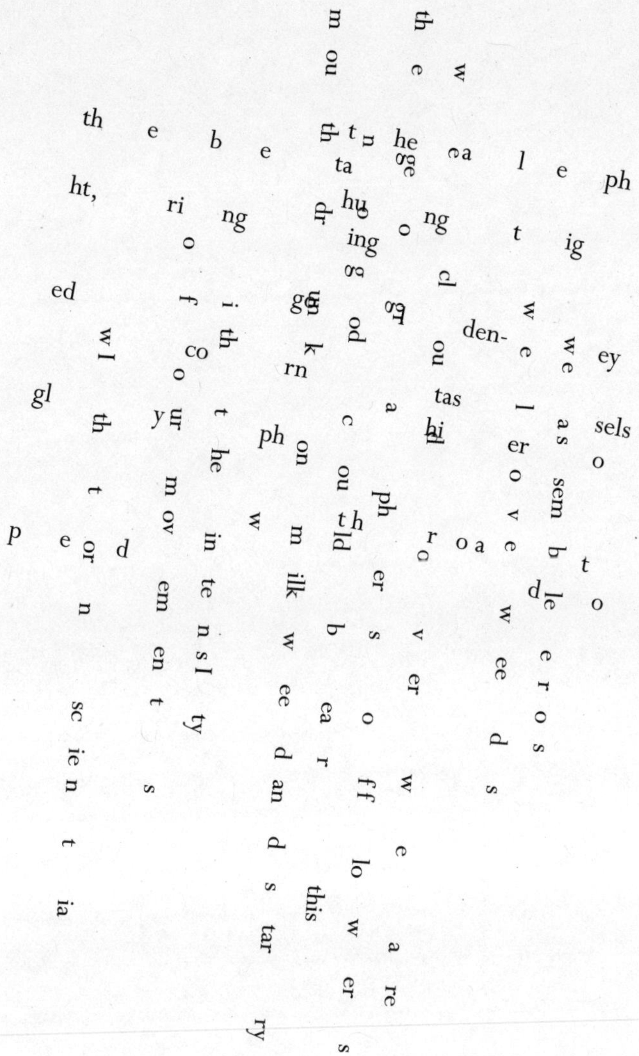

THE

Be/s of the Invisible

THE BE/S OF THE INVISIBLE

A BIO-SEMIOTICS

BEE FLIGHT AS SCRIPT: THE WAGGLE DANCE, THE ROUND DANCE AND FORAGING

"we are the bees of the Invisible" — RILKE

from a collaborative performance on colony collapse disorder and the necessary beauty of bees with pianist and ethnomusicologist Kumi Uyeda using trumpet, piano, accordion, tonkori toy piano, melodica, live and recorded voices, electronic music, video and projections at Flytrap Studio, Oakland

"we
could
not imagine
that solid flesh
might float in space
nor that the rough landscape
we saw around us might compose
only the merest fraction, or glimpse,
of an immense luminescent Body,
a shape as perfect and boundless
as a sphere, spinning"

DAVID ABRAM, *BECOMING ANIMAL*

the swarm articulates

the sex of a soul

its flower-rhyme

divination by the viscera of words

cumulous,

tremulous

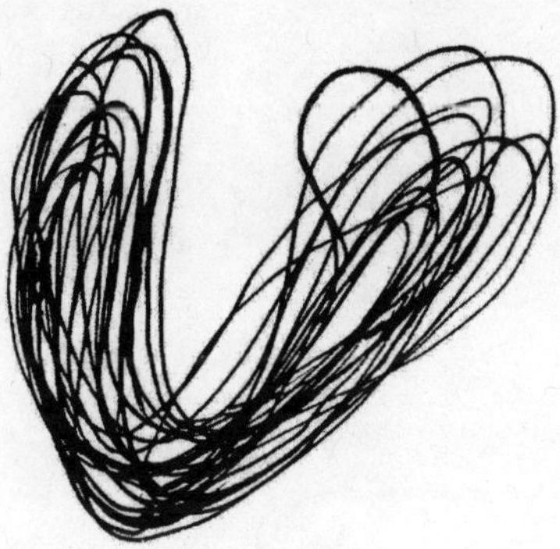

"this tiny, insect life the portal to another" — EMILY DICKINSON

ALEPH, BETA

we are the secret
pinned to a vortex
raptured with torn scientia
our little hands
the aleph, the beta
hungtight, ringing
gone o o o o
gone away home
bound golden-
eyed
corn tassels
hieroglyph
throat
doped

WE ARE THE RIVETERS OF POLLEN

feeling our way by our leg hairs
and the ultra-violet sensors in our eyes
we hover we come apart we are gold rivers our eyes shine
we assemble eros
we love weeds
we are the geographers of flowers
we translate petals

OUR WINGS REFRACT CLOUDS

we hover we come apart
in precise relation to the sun no god could bear this
mouth drunk on milkweed
a low beating noise   starry with the intensity of our movements
our leg hairs unimaginably sensitive and sticky

WHAT IF WE ARE THE LANGUAGE OF OTHERS

what if
language is
both inside
and outside the body
intra-species, polyphonic
what if we are the words
others' mouths cannot form
without us
sparks set loose like bees glistening
selva oscura
dark woods dark words
frayed, sentient
sensorium harmonium
brokered
borders
she throws open her hands
into raw unsewn
air

IN FIELDS OF THE MISSING

in the brittle
uncanny silence
of empty white
hive boxes
do you remember
birds arboreal
in quantum
oceans of air hymning
discarded containers of Gaucho™
pesticide the dark
matter of hands
our ghost shirt
and ghost wind
our ghost dirt
to prophesy
ghost profit
wanton bereft
do you remember
flowering that swept
your eyes
awake
it was shame
        that lit me
            like a flame
              to keep stumbling
                 and pretending not to
              in the ache
          of bluebirds grassland

HIS GOLDEN PELT

Beo-wulf, bee-man, little bison
monegum mægþum meodo-setla oftēah into the mead-
hall he plunges
with his shining axe
his scarred and golden pelt his bright swarm
his interstate bees, fossil fuel bees
bees with guns, bees with suns
transported like Minutemen missiles
across prairies and test-sites

nothing that is not Being
or being rinsed through with dark excess my mouth
confused with night

FLOWERS THAT BELONG TO THE DEAD

flowers that unclothe their bodies
without reserve
gone glottal and feral, outside our focus
our everyday lives in late summer orchards
blank stare of the sun
"the chemical warfare that is modern agriculture"
pink plastic toys lined up in the rain

[1] multi-national clothianidin dust in our furrows coating seed-corn and soybeans

[2] nearly invisible in living aquifers and the pollen hair of disoriented bees who join the disappeared of the Plaza de las Madres and those missing on reconnaissance over napalmed Agent Orange rice-fields, over *terra roxa*, the raw purple soil of Amazonia

[3] coincidence of agricultural products and weapons: Agents Orange, Blue and White were all first used as herbicides

THE OPEN

"and yet

sometimes

a silent animal looks up at us

and silently looks through us"

ring-neck snake your coral flower

your dragonfly blue

your tiny furred bees your wild

countenance swims dusk coyotes

ecstatic as maenads

weft, reft   womb

hulled   drunk on

our futures

virtual

hunger

stroking the hair of my bees

transparency of their flight, opacity of desire

FREE RADICAL

without permission
happiness happens
or flesh-eating bacteria
sudden flash in near
and far conifers
the excessive yellow
and scarlet of a tanager
why so bright
unless Beauty
is hell-bent
upon existing
despite survival
of the fittest
automobile
free-market
autocracy
in hedgerows
hedge funds
all life
hinges

forever is a dream a nightmare
like heaven, a chasm

SENTIENT BEING

because the body
is a ladder
of incomparable pain
this is burning
as I speak
because the body is a ladder
of living forests, animals and rain
they ran, scattered and ran
but not fast enough
because the body is a ladder
of incomparable pain because the body
cannot outrun
loss of sustenance and sun
woven with oracular bees, trembling
awaken bees, arise bees, trembling
tongue to tongue, the colors, trembling
whose yellow bodies soar, trembling
cast off into the open, perilous
pollen-filled air
where gods or God erased the populations
not gods or God
our war-heads
our petrochemical
scrubbed data
ethnically clean
the stars on fire

BELOVED

your mouth of dust turned gold your mouth
of nothing your mouth of heterotrophic birds set free

beloved, there is

no blossom-skin nor Eden yellowinged

no bios without thee

THE LANGUAGE OF BEES

HAZARDOUS materials

"what is the purpose
of resisting corporate globalization
if not to protect the obscure, the ineffable, the unmarketable
...the local, the poetic, and the eccentric?"

REBECCA SOLNIT

SHOCK

"B Redemption
1 Shock
a Extinguished semblance
b Veiling of beauty
c Nakedness
2 Hope"

WALTER BENJAMIN
NOTES FOR ELECTIVE AFFINITIES

they closed
the bridge for toxic spillage
people out in the gritty refinery air
looking down at yellow barges
there is very little we know that can surpass
the achievement of spiders
or how acutely Bill Viola's camera sees into
the eyes of an owl or the sad presence of
"biologically active quantities of common
over-the-counter and prescription drugs (e.g. Prozac)
ubiquitous in European and North American
urban and suburban waste waters
where discharge to streams and rivers
wreaks havoc on aquatic
endocrine systems"
the horizon lies down
like a tired
animal

WHAT
TO KEEP
IN MIND

the necessity
and constant upheaval
of Heraclitean flux
recombinant pre-Socratic
elements gas liquid solid etcetera
transmigrating verb, tense, gender
and do not forget
the auditorium of bees, the audibleness of bees
the many forms love takes
light through coral peony petals
light through cortex
all the systems burning, all the systems
hived wide-open by
C NAKEDNESS
2 HOPE
do not leave out the rawness
the Veiling of beauty

lost in twigs, "cured" of language, unfinished and starry

HUE [AWE]

"Threnodies] Extacies - /
Revenues - / *Arguments*"

EMILY DICKINSON, VARIANTS 671,634,637

seen
from another planet
there is
not much difference
between people and amoebas
ocean or ice floes
between a cloud
and a transistor radio
however, each makes noise
with light differently
each bears the marks
of accident in its own way
you are not as lost as you thought
you are globally positioned
you occupy the exact intersection
of a million grass blades
where a spider is a meadow
a calling, a brink
and the air is ringing
against the slightly bitter
scent of wisteria in a small blue glass bowl
the ingredients for bombs readily available on the internet
what vast intimacy we share

THE END OF THE WORLD

has already happened
is happening
here it is
what to prove
nothing other than
the small coiled teeth
of mollusk radulae scraping
granite tidepools clean
seen correctly
every bush
is a burning bush

GRAVITATION

"all in all/ nothing in one part, as fluid, ether, or such like/
-analogy of this to soul, to consciousness / that nothing-something,
something-nothing"

COLERIDGE, NOTEBOOKS

stepping
toward meltdown
I sit on a clearing
favored by grass snakes
weather is their motion
a blossom in the mouth of each snake's
purple-black tongue
I'm taking pleasure in infinitesimals, drawn
to the unfinished, the impossible to finish, resistant
scraps half-eaten, scratched out tracks
or scat scattered, reprocessed mouse bones
gnawed manzanita berries
blinded, blindsided
as in entering brightness from the dark
don't imagine there is another paradise than this
lost place, nothing split off
from God's blowback, nor apparent disregard
nor love left out
in the open

LET GOLDFINCHES FLY OUT OF YELLOW

wild mustard
let the sun rotate
as though seeming to circle the earth
let rain fall into storm culverts
and the blue dragonfly
swerve out of blue sky
begin to count the beats of your heart
then uncount them
imitate a tree then imitate
a tree imitating you
then forget which one you are
now arrange crows to reflect sky
with their wings
and then chainsaws
to wail across the canyon
like lost
souls

AWAKE

“October 18, 1917.
Dread of night. Dread of not-night.”

KAFKA, THE BLUE OCTAVO NOTEBOOKS

everyone I love is dying
everything I love is dying
beauty crosses
black
sea air
chasm

CLOUDS

open
and close
ceaselessly
at the sound of a fly
who probes the light like Mallarmé
we have exchanged places and now I live
within the white and black and deep orange of its keep
regarding myself with the compound eyes of a fly
outside the realm of care or sleep
the invisible is on fire and not one flower
will survive its own opening
though flowering
persists like a flame
held stuttering
in wild
unshielded
air

IN VAST FLIGHTS

"after this I saw starlings in vast flights, borne along like smoke, mist… expanding, or contracting, thinning or condensing, now glimmering and shivering, now thickening, deepening, blackening"

COLERIDGE, NOTEBOOKS

we pass
each other
on the street
privatized
this one and the next
sudden god
extinction
borne along
like tidal drift
reborn as avatar or code
we could be human
we could be contrails
we take the form of foxes
in the Samara region of the Volga
responding to the scent of rodents
or their movement under the snow
we stop and prick up our ears
we wait, we stalk or leap
our commingled
territorial proprioception
alert to the slightest
tremor of
leaves

NAKED
NESS

encrypted
isolate
raveled in self-similar
species waves
we are extremely attached
to each personal
electronic device
passing each other on the street
this person and the next
incantatory lost flower
simultaneous in our
non-linear flocks
we are extremely
attached
ear to ear
air of earth
your new-born mind
in solidarity
with living
things
a car door
slams
shut

a n e m o c h o r e

plant that spreads seeds or fruit by wind

adj. *anemochorous* / wind chorus dithyrambic
polyspecies lyric

"*Umwelt*...

the skein that every animal forms for itself by winding itself into the world according to its means, with its nervous system, its senses, its shape, its tools, its mobility"

JEAN-CHRISTOPHE BAILLY

I go out *Umwelted* like Joseph Beuys wrapped in felt, field of night
grasses on fire that unweld, then reweld me in hieroglyphs of light
I go out in my skein, my bright skin of world a planetary nervous system
netted in "mazy movement" and green ardor, net worth decimated by
photosynthetic dollars, even the rich at risk their "senses" their "tools"
their "mobility" likened to ants who've lost their trail of scent

the sweat

of belonging

all these other humans

burning

in kindred

are you a wind instrument are you breath
gone wild, running are you once a tree now
aswarm, aswim in the orchard of bees
I am constantly made aware that words are teaching me
that I am inside *their* mouth

some of us would like our bodies to become a meadow
whose order is wild where a word is its own translation
nature tries to love us but sometimes cannot
/ find a way / through

language is an animal it howls flees hides and waits watches us to see
if we'll come to our senses in red algae bloom fluorescence or flake flake
flake of plucked pelt pelagic pleading calm then kneeling
"wings stuck fast in the burning glue"

the branch so dark against her skin

how fierce its sap

pure distance given its rawness

unlikeness

this time Hermes false rib fallow deer "yellowish coat spotted
in summer" not quite overlapping as in imbricate pine cone scales
or turtle shell in case of emergency you can build a cave in leaf-blowers
irreparable | reparation

tessellate

hate crime

red meat

my appetite

X billions

your interior my interior the wilderness' interior inside a word
the interior is vast, each cloud erasing then forming ecstatic rainwater
I'm breathing your oxygen you're breathing my carbon dioxide
green world blue world red world my darling permeable membrane
there is no greater love than this
folded in involutes

cast into

swarming

Incomplete, as now I

before you

language is an animal it howls in wind-tunnel blood vessels mute raw
fractal fraternal no other habitat than our mouths meadowed
in solitude and contrailed surveilled surplus populations
o it listens and waits for the unbought *Logos* of mothers
standing in line with their flagrant
tenderness

how Field
\ overlaps

Nothing
by itself

“separation” “fence” or “security” “fence” with “seam zones”
or “racial segregation” “wall” “apartheid wall” or “acceptable” “generic”
“descriptions” such as “barrier” which the “International” “Court”
of “Justice” refers to as “wall” since “other” “expressions” “sometimes”
“employed” “are no more” “accurate” “if understood”
“in the” “physical sense”

immune system run amok in aquifers homeland

no-fly zones

in the physical sense

give me your hand rinse off your shoulders then rotate like a solar system

like a heliotrope try to find some surface of your self that doesn't touch

marshlands war-heads starfish littoral living systems ceaselessly refuse

to abandon us even when annihilation presents tense edge of

cellular lucidity

head out into the Open with ten words from John Cage as compass
forms of biomimicry as urban tidepools and structures we invent
and breathe collapse then compost ourselves
I am willing

it is "just a mess" —beauty

I've lost your trail again

interior life of words

dendritic and fractal

“THE WHOLE SEA
of me burning”

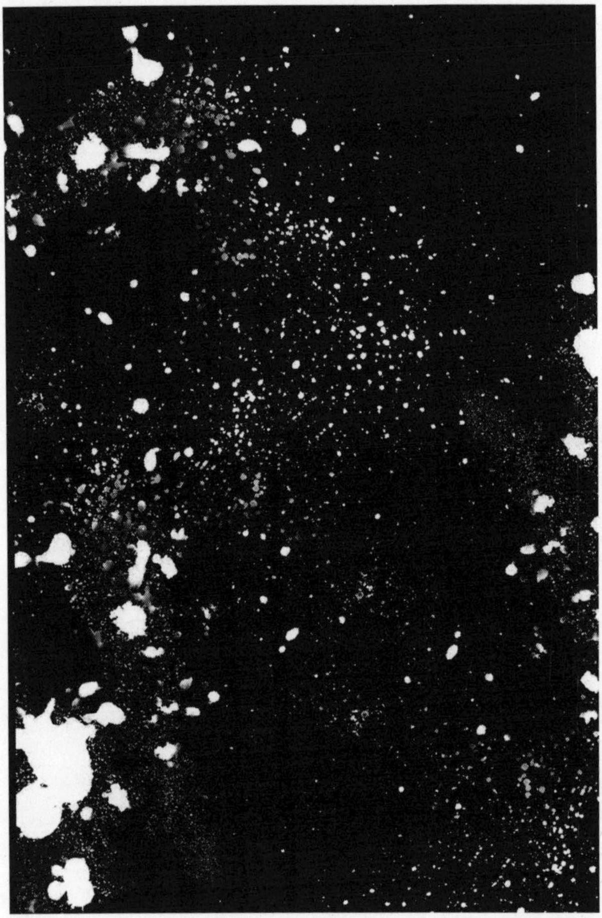

THE WHOLE SEA OF ME

reading an echo of Mary Shelley today: "the whole sea of me burning"
& words are flames, our eyes also

the whole sea hammering
the whole sea molten
trees explode on far ridges
across from our living room
splinters of flame
sunlight burned orange
canyons like torches
space and time on fire
chaparral cities on fire
freeways on fire
fire on fire
schist on fire
feathers of flame
stampedes of flame
a crow caws in your throat
this world and the next poised
on the edge of its wing

DEEPWATER, TRUTH & BEAUTY

*"Many had been asleep when the blast occurred,
and wandered the slick, debris-strewn deck, shoeless,
clad in little more than their orange life jackets,
their bare skin speckled with bits of white insulation
from blown-out walls."*

APRIL 20, 2010, DEEP HORIZON OIL RIG

A FISHERMAN CRIES OUT
"the water's on fire, dude"
cries out "the water's on fire"
the water IS ON FIRE
right now

many had been asleep
while our lives were uploaded
and shared and liked or unliked,
we were seabirds on kelpbeds
our wings felt the air
without paranoia or pain
without payment
or debt or doubt
many earths
ago

IS TRUTH | BEAUTY

or the other way around, is death beautiful
because it is true, am I beautiful, am I true
are my words beautiful, is truth beautiful
covered in oil, are facts true enough
to burn, beautiful enough to burn
in the realm of fish and humans

"as safe as before the spill" according to BP Oil

well, there is not one animal who believes this
not one songbird in a willow
tree at dawn, not one deafened whale
or red snapper in shoals not one foal
or snake or sea cucumber starfish or radish no river-mouth
or fractal shore-break nor any polynuclear aromatic hydrocarbon
released during the explosion during the spill during
the dispersants not one spark of carbon
from one burned out star

THE RIG

deepwater-horizon oil-rig 21:56 4.20.2010
http://www.youtube.com/watch?v=8OegAlLnPLs&feature=fvwrel

SPLIT

-second

turbine,

Lady

gone a/

sunder Ga-Ga ®

their poor mouths

in which sea creatures

and workers

no warnings of

waterfire

®

unconscious

give air in shocked geologic

dreamt of their beauty

engines to run

nor could have anyone

predicted

"entirely" "contained"

I jump into

fiery water

"black-eyed"

"angels"

"swam with me"

the acts of water, the speech of water

I cannot stay away

"his tar-smeared hair"

a mirror

for mind to consecrate

where dolphins leap

and silver the air

skins changed and new legs, or no legs   at gulfstream feeding stations
not rage, something more lasting
soul roaring like a hurricane over shoddy tax-cut levees

"Hear how #BP's technology team created to help minimize #oilspill damage and aid cleanup: http://bit.ly/bYXI54 *about 1 hour ago"*

"Check out how #BP creates #biofuels in our interactive animation: http://bit.ly/BiofuelsAnimation"

"Eyeless shrimp, fish with sores, deformed sea life: today's Gulf of Mexico: http://www.foxnews.com/scitech/2012/04/18/eyeless-shrimp-and-mutant-fish-raise-concerns-over-bp-spill-effects/ thanks #BP" Michael Betancourt@Cinegraphic

"#BREAKING: #BP (@BP_America) BP trying to get away with less than one tenth of what it really owes for disaster http://www.huffingtonpost.com/antonia-juhasz/bp-oil-settlement_b_1583520.html"

"Will you be attending this weekend's World Championship Gumbo Cook-Off in New Iberia?" http://bit.ly/cVBI8p *8 minutes ago*

Will you enter "seafood," "chicken and sausage" or "mélange" categories
Will you be participant or observer, lobbied or rented, consumed or consumer
Will you be paired with a beverage or "covered in sores"

DIATOMS RISING

"Microscopic one-celled creatures known as diatoms are thought to be the source of a vast majority of the world's oil."

NY TIMES

"Everything becomes fire, and from fire everything is born, as in the eternal exchange of money and merchandise"

HERACLITUS, FRAGMENT 28

let Bios rise up — every rhizomic spore
        and comrade diatoms shaped like sputnik satellites
                like emoji who refuse to wear pleasant, human faces
                        let diatoms rise up and rhyme the Truth of Beauty
                                in the markets of a living world

CORAL REEF

"It was love that moves me and love makes me speak"
BEATRICE, INFERNO, CANTO II

I look away, people are coming, birds shatter cypress and sky
another species falls null, is that fate acting upon us, are our eyes ever
open enough, it is an ordinary day, that's what you think and then
you are gone, he is gone, a brain tumor, fever, a wound, three weeks
later, she is gone, the earth opens up, the earth is generous
abiding in cascades of loss, hiding in oceans of disappearance

it was love that moves me and scatters me and casts me forth as a flock
of starlings far beyond mind's breakwater

to say "I exist" is also to ask
"am I a fiction"
for I cannot read my book
it reads me instead
in the spreading sheen of oil
in the cusp of evening
in the roar of traffic the voice
of a boy selling cellophaned roses
to vehicles that speed past him
light-years away
the luminous combines
the infinite kindnesses
orphaned in oil
in our matrix of wetlands and reef
desert and grief, every animal
is perishable, permeable

now that time is no longer
infinite and the future is
no longer paradise
there is another kind of music
another kind of noise
you work with forms that approximate
the crowding and overlapping of habitat borders
where species collide, co-exist, entangled
with the spillage of human imagination, desires, conflict
scarcity, the effluence of borders, bones, biomes
those left behind, the unmade
beds of internment camps
accelerated evolution
air crammed with wireless
polyphony of untethered
weathers where we are the score
that is writing us
no different than kelp beds
or forests or elk herds

DEAR ANIMAL,

you have ten minutes to draw a life
kindred, like a coral reef

maybe ten seconds, take your time

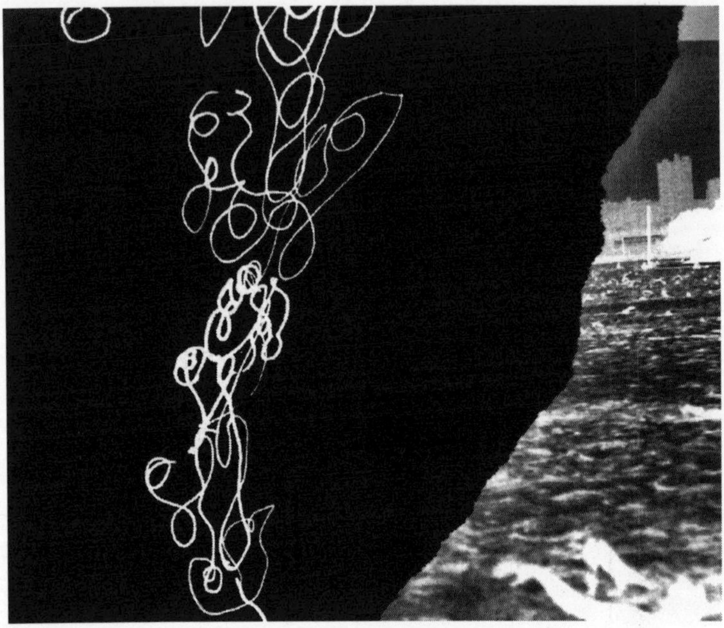

"I'd wanted friends
Who talked of a public justice"

GEORGE OPPEN

WHAT are poets for

YOUR CORAL FLOWER

PERFORMANCE DOCUMENTS FOR THE BE/S OF THE INVISIBLE

INSTRUCTIONS FOR AUDIENCE AND PERFORMERS

1. open your envelope
2. read aloud the entire text at your own pace
3. when you come to a number, pause for the number of seconds shown
for example: "3" means a three second pause
4. use your own sense of timing — everyone will be reading
at a different pace
5. feel free to move around the space as a hive/swarm
6. begin when signaled

awaken bees, arise bees, trembling [1]
tongue to tongue, the colors, trembling [4]
the waggle dance, the round dance [1]
threw open her hands into raw unsewn [5]
nothing that is not Being or being rinsed through with dark excess
my mouth [9] woven with oracular bees, trembling [7]
feeling our way by our leg hairs and the ultra-violet sensors [1]
in the fields of the missing [2] dark matter of hands [5]
our everyday lives [9] in late summer orchards [4]
stroking the hair of my bees [8]
we buy nothing we sell nothing we hover [12]
into the mead-hall he plunges [10]
you are the secret pinned to a vortex [7]
interstate bees, fossil fuel bees [5]
tongue to tongue, the colors, trembling [16]
ring-neck snake your coral flower your dragonfly blue [9]
islands your tiny furred bees your wild …

th

we as ed sem gl b le e r o s

w ht, l o v e w ee d s

ph ey sels o t o

w e ig cl ou d d o v er

e w e er a re

th e l t ge o den- gr a o a ph er s o

a ng ff tas lo hi w er s

n he o g od c ou ld b ea r

this t h

t hu

m ou th dr go rn un k on m ilk w ee

ta ing d an d s tar ry w

i th t he in te n s I ty

o e f o ur co m ov em en t s

ph d

b ng w I th t or n

sc ie n e t ri ia e

y p

alternate between chanting and reading the performance text

chant phonemically where noted

WHAT ARE POETS FOR

what are poets for
what are poets for
what are poets for
in a destitute time?
in a destitute time?
what are poets for
in a destitute time?
in a destitute time?

leaves on water that move like dolphins

a quantity of people expressing nationhood wounds

we are not different and not the same

late sun afternoon lakeside: we are Whitman's grasses

the ways I love
hate you

includes
cancels us
deports
erases

many beautiful faces standing before a flag that

quickly enspirited

at risk

SUCH AS BIRD SOUNDS

The phrases in YOUR CORAL FLOWER were randomly selected and arranged as a composition by Kumi Uyeda using quotations from the performance text THE BE/S OF THE INVISIBLE

- toward creating performance that is inclusive, multi-vocal, sensorial, transformative

- altering the passive consumer role of audience members into co-creators where sound and movement are generated from the audience as well as those on stage

- the hope is to communalize poetry when the locus of voice shuttles between poet and audience, word and world as co-created process

- to experience and extend poetry beyond the cerebral by engaging body, ethics, action, movement in full sensory biosphere

"Utterances, then, are more variable, less constrained, and 'messier' than the concept they express ... there will be a great variation in how any particular utterance of a word such as *bird* sounds"

EDUARDO KOHN, *HOW FORESTS THINK: TOWARD AN ANTHROPOLOGY BEYOND THE HUMAN*

Is the soul more political than we have ever conceived?

Acknowledgments

Words are living beings. I am aware that these pages and images arise from words that are alive and carry their own knowledge. They move through me, through all of us, like a river, though countless speakers, human and non-human, present or lost to memory. These pages are made from places and encounters where I have walked and dreamed to reconvene here — the beings of meadows, shorelines, clouds, people, bees, cities, hummingbirds, hawks, coyotes, grasses. We share the beauty, contamination and the precipice of disappearance with our world in intimate, precarious kinship.

With gratitude to the publishers, editors, curators and musicians who encouraged this work and carried it into public space, at times in earlier versions, in print, performance & mixed-media formats:

Allies: A Literary Anthology (Boston Review/MIT Press)	from DO ANIMALS DREAM "dear animate" "the brightness of the animal" "when rivers are granted personhood"
Boston Review online and audio *Boston Review* Poetry Prize finalist	DO ANIMALS DREAM
Conjunctions: 64/Natural Causes	ANEMOCHORE
Conjunctions online 02.11.14.	THE BE/S: A BIOSEMIOTICS with a series of color performance projection stills

The Volta—Evening Will Come #59 *Insect Poetics*	"the swarm articulates"
The Iowa Review, Iowa Review Poetry Prize	from HAZARDOUS MATERIALS "shock" "what to keep in mind" "[Hue] Awe" "the end of the world" "gravitation" "let goldfinches fly out of yellow" "awake" "in vast flights"
Poetry Daily	"the end of the world" "let goldfinches fly out of yellow"
mistake, Caketrain chapbook	STARS ARE BEING also performed and recorded with Kumi Uyeda on piano and tonkori
Tupelo Quarterly	from WHAT ARE POETS FOR "your coral flower" "what are poets for?" "such as bird sounds" "is the soul more political than we have ever conceived?"

The series ANEMOCHORE and THE BE/S OF THE INVISIBLE are included in the chapbook *anemochore*, winner of the Gloria Anzaldúa prize from Newfound Press

anemochore was a finalist for the 2019 Four Quartets Prize from the Poetry Society of America and the T. S. Eliot Foundation

The image/text "Is the soul more political than we ever imagined?" appeared online in *BAX: Best American Experimental Writing*, Wesleyan University Press

"When rivers are granted personhood" also appeared in the chapbook *By here, by there, by when, by while* from the Emerging Narratives Working Group, sponsored by the USC Levan Institute for the Humanities

THE BE/S OF THE INVISIBLE was first performed at Flytrap Studio in Oakland. I want to express my gratitude, wide as the night sky, to Kumi Uyeda and Kallan Nishimoto at FLYTRAP STUDIO for their continuing intersection of music, art, dance, poetry, performance, inventive and unexpected collaborations creating community, solidarity and the spaciousness of the new.

Notes

The Open : "*...bound to the mystery of their existence, contained as it was in the nets of all other existences*"

JEAN-CHRISTOPHE BAILLY

DO ANIMALS DREAM

"Do Animals Dream?" title of article by Liz Langley, *National Geographic*

"embedded in the visible..." Jean-Christophe Bailly, *The Animal Side*

"the young emaciated..." refers to rookeries of brown pelicans on Raccoon Island in the Gulf after the BP oil spill. See "5 Years After BP Oil Spill, Effects Linger and Recovery Is Slow," Debbie Elliot, NPR

"the sentence, a sentence" Ingeborg Bachmann, *Darkness Spoken*

"when rivers are granted personhood" see "The Legal Personality of Rivers" EMA blog from http://www.emahumanrights.org/2019/01/16/the-legal-personality-of-rivers/

THE BE/S OF THE INVISIBLE

"we could not imagine..." David Abram, *Becoming Animal*

Nancy Spero's paintings and murals echo in this work

"the chemical warfare..." from Desert Scientist, dailykos.com

"And yet sometimes an animal looks up..." Rilke

HAZARDOUS MATERIALS

The selection from WALTER BENJAMIN, *NOTES FOR ELECTIVE AFFINITIES* is quoted from Walter Benjamin, *Archive*. Edited by Ursula Marx, Gudrun Schwarz, Michael Schwarz, Erdmut Wizisla "biologically active quantities..." from Stephen Meyer, "End of the Wild" *Boston Review*, April 2004

The Complete Poems of Emily Dickinson, edited by Thomas H. Johnson

"you are a fox..." based on the study "Signal Field Theory In Ecological Semiotics" E. Vladimirova, J. Mozgovoy

For more on phase shifts and murmurations: see "Starling Flock Networks Manage Uncertainty in Consensus at Low Cost" George F. Young, Luca Scardovi, Andrea Cavagna, Irene Giardina, Naomi E. Leonard in *PLOS Computational Biology*, 2013, http://journals.plos.org/ploscompbiol/article?id=10.1371/journal.pcbi.1002894

"after this I saw starlings..." Samuel Coleridge in *Coleridge's Notebooks: A Selection*

On the sentience of starling murmurations and other phase shifts see *Wonderopolis* (http://wonderopolis.org/wonder/what-is-a-murmuration) Murmurations are now believed to act like phase shifts – phenomena whose interconnected elements are tuned to work in unison and in relation to each other: "Scientists believe murmurations are similar to other systems, such as crystals forming, avalanches, metals becoming magnetized and liquids turning to gases. These systems are 'on the edge,' which means they're ready to be completely transformed in an instant. Like the elements of these other systems, each starling in a murmuration is connected to every other starling ... when a murmuration turns in unison, scientists believe it's like a phase transition."

I am also indebted to the endlessly fertile use of fractal forms in the bilaterally centered poems in Michael McClure's *Of Indigo and Saffron*, edited by Leslie Scalapino

ANEMOCHORE

"mazy movement" Ronald Johnson, *The Book of the Green Man*

"separation" "fence" ... "Israeli West Bank Barrier," "names of the barrier," Wikipedia https://en.wikipedia.org/wiki/Israeli_West_Bank_barrier#Names_of_the_barrier

"wings stuck fast in the burning glue" Dante, *Inferno*, Canto XXII, translated by Susan Mitchell from *Dante's Inferno: Translations by 20 Contemporary Poets*, edited by Daniel Halpern

"ten words from John Cage" used in print-making process, *Every Day is a Good Day: The Visual Art of John Cage:* Introduction by Roger Malbert, text by Jeremy Millar, Lauren A. Wright, Helen Luckett

"it's just a mess" John Cage

THE WHOLE SEA OF ME BURNING

"the whole sea of me..." a quotation as though attributed to Mary Shelley from Laurie Sheck, *A Monster's Notes*

"It was love..." Dante, *Inferno*, edited by Daniel Halpern, Canto II, translated by Seamus Heaney

"many had been asleep..." "Inferno on the Gulf: 'This is the real deal!'; for survivors, a night of horror and sorrow" by Allen Breed and Kevin McGill, Associated Press Writers, www.ap.org/oil_spill/Recount_61010.html

"the water's on fire" from youtube video posted by local fisherman "Knightriderz" at the scene of the Deepwater explosion: http://www.youtube.com/watch?v=8OEgAlLnPLs&feature=fvwrel

THE RIG is roughly patterned after Mallarmé's "*Un Coup de Dés Jamais N'abolira le Hasard*"

"black-eyed angels" adapted from Radiohead's *Pyramid Song*

"his tar-smeared..." Dante, *Inferno*, edited by Daniel Halpern, from Canto XXII translated by Susan Mitchell "*as safe as before the spill...*" from BP claims posted at dailykos.com

"Microscopic one-celled creatures..." "Tracing Oil Reserves to Their Tiny Origins," William Broad; *New York Times* http://www.nytimes.com/2010/08/03/science/03oil.html

WHAT ARE POETS FOR

"What are poets for in a destitute time?" Heidegger quoting Hölderlin in *Poetry, Language, Thought*

IMAGES

Cover image: Thom Cowen

Illustrations are by the author or in the author's collection, except for the diatom drawing in THE WHOLE SEA OF ME BURNING by Ernst Haeckel, in the Public domain *via Wikimedia Commons*, re-worked by the author

MEREDITH STRICKER is the author of six poetry collections and recipient of the National Poetry Series Award, the Omnidawn Open Book Award and the Tupelo Press Dorset Prize. Her work involves performance, drawing, graphic overlays and hybrid forms of documentary/lyric. She explores a sentient world through media ranging from paint and ink to artist books and buildings. As an artist, designer and poet, she co-directs POETICS AND SPACE a collaborative that focuses on architecture in Big Sur, along with projects to bring together artists, writers, musicians and experimental forms.

Her poetry and visual work have appeared widely in journals as well as in galleries and performance spaces including *Conjunctions, The Boston Review*, *Best American Experimental Writing*, and *The Iowa Review*. Other awards include the Australian Book Review Poetry Prize, Gloria Anzaldúa Award, the Iowa Review Poetry Award, the Emily Dickinson Award and finalist for the Four Quartets prize from the Poetry Society of America.

SENTIENCE
by Meredith Stricker
Cover art by Thom Cowen
Cover font: Aptos

Interior design by Laura Joakimson and Meredith Stricker
Interior typefaces: Perpetua and Minion

Printed in the United States by Books International,
Dulles, Virginia on Acid Free Archival Quality Recycled Paper

Publication of this book was made possible in part by gifts from
Katherine & John Gravendyk in honor of Hillary Gravendyk,
Francesca Bell, Mary Mackey, and The New Place Fund

Omnidawn Publishing
Oakland, California